WHY CAT WHY
a coloring book explaining cats

drawn and written by
Theo Nicole Lorenz

ISBN 978-0-9975738-4-8

This book is dedicated to cats

Every single cat

But since cats can't read
please pet a cat for me
and pass along my love

Cats might seem mysterious, but we can explain
why cats are the way they are.

Cats sleep on your laptop to block your view
of the comments section. YOU'RE WELCOME.

Cats get underfoot to help you exercise.
It's leg day!

It's difficult to get up when a cat is on you because cat gravity is three times as strong as Earth's gravity.

De-cluttering gives cats a sense of control
in a chaotic, ever-changing world.

Cats sleep like that because they don't have dignity.
Or bones.

Cats' early warning signals go off
when a food bowl reaches half capacity.

Cats are required by law to update you about their buttholes.
If you don't like butt updates, contact your legislators.

Cats chew on cords to steal electricity for their laser eyes.

Cats zoom around after pooping because
they're trying to outrun the evil they've unleashed.

Cats are nature's supervisors!
LET CAT HELP YOU.

Cats are very particular about fashion,
and you are ruining their aesthetic!

In the wild, the vacuum cleaner is a cat's natural predator.

In case of emergency, your cat has filled itself with warmth from sunbeams and can function as a heater.

Your cat pooped in those shoes to save you from wearing them on your date. Seriously, Sharon, what were you thinking?

Cats like to lie in the sink because
being close to danger makes them feel alive.

Pointiness is the way cats say "I love you."

Cats make otherworldly noises because they're aliens from meowter space and that's how they call the meowthership.

Cats drink from the paint water cup because...
honestly, we don't know. It's gross. HEY, STOP THAT!

Cats...are a mystery.

How are cats so precious?
Some questions science cannot answer.

What did we do to deserve cats?

It's okay to love something that doesn't make sense.

Cats don't understand you,
but they love you back anyway.

Cats are weird. You should get one.

About the Artist

Theo sometimes cries because they love their cats so much. Said cats are Moby, an elderly trash mammal, and October Von Spoopypants, an enormous throw pillow.

Theo is the artist behind several unusual coloring books, including *Unicorns Are Jerks: a coloring book exposing the cold, hard, sparkly truth,* and *The Robot's Guide to Love: a coloring book of romantic advice.*

Find more of Theo's stuff at TheoNicole.com!

Special thanks to Whitney and her cat Emma, who starred in the last page.

CPSIA information can be obtained
at www.ICGtesting.com
Printed in the USA
LVHW06s2333010518
575645LV00032B/456/P

9 780997 573848